SHAPING THE EARTH
EROSION

BY SANDRA DOWNS

Twenty-First Century Books
Brookfield, Connecticut

To Dave
For his help, support, and appreciation
of scenic geologic features

Published by Twenty-First Century Books
A Division of The Millbrook Press, Inc.
2 Old New Milford Road
Brookfield, Connecticut 06804
www.millbrookpress.com

Library of Congress Cataloging-in-Publication Data
Downs, Sandra.
Shaping the Earth/Sandra Downs.
p. cm–(Exploring planet earth)
Includes bibliographical references.
Summary: Examines the different forces of erosion, such as wind, waves, acid rain, and glaciers, explains how they affect the topography of the earth, and describes their results, including dust storms, sand dunes, and caves.
ISBN 0-7613-1414-8 (lib. bdg.)
1. Erosion–Juvenile literature. [1. Erosion] I. Title II. Series.
QE571.D68 2000
551.3'02–dc21   99-045541

Cover photograph courtesy of Photo Researchers, Inc. (© Richard Hansen)

Photographs courtesy of Visuals Unlimited: pp. 8 (© Gerald & Buff Corsi), 11 (© Nada Pecnik), 46 (© 1992 G.L.E.); Transparencies, Inc.: p. 10 (© Mike Booher); © 1998 Sandra Downs: p. 13; Peter Arnold, Inc.: p. 16 (© James G. Wark); Animals Animals/Earth Scenes: pp. 17 (© Eastcott/Momatiuk), 19 (© Michael Fogden), 29 (© Roger W. Archibald), 32 (© Francis Lepine), 38 (© Bertram G. Murray, Jr.), 44 (© C. C. Lockwood); U.S.G.S.: pp. 18 (D. E. Trimble, 12ct); © James A. Pisarowicz: p. 21; Photo Researchers, Inc.: pp. 23 (© Kenneth Murray), 34 (© Mark Newman), 36 (© Mark Newman), 51 (© Earl Roberge); Lackawanna Historical Society: p. 24; NGS Image Collection: p. 25 (© Richard Nowitz); Liaison Agency: p. 26 (© Anthony Suau); NASA: p. 42; National Park Service, White Sands National Monument: p. 45; USDA-Soil Conservation Service: p. 48

CONTENTS

SHAPING
THE EARTH
EROSION

PREFACE

Pick up a handful of soil, and breathe in its earthy aroma. Pick up a handful of sand, and let it run through your fingers. Once upon a time, those grains of sand and those soft bits of soil sat perched on a mountaintop, or on a cliff along a wave-swept shore. But all mighty mountains eventually crumble into grains of sand—thanks to erosion, the earth's most powerful landscaper!

By breaking down and carrying away rocks, erosion recycles the earth's surface. Quartz, quartzite, and sandstone disintegrate into sand. Feldspar turns into clay. Clay crumbles into tiny particles of silt. Take these particles, mix in a heaping helping of humus (decayed plants and animals), and presto—it's soil! Packed full of mineral nutrients from its rock components, soil is the ground we walk on, the dirt we take for granted. It's a critical part of our lives, since without soil there are no crops. And without crops, we have no food. By slowly churning rocks into particles, erosion provides us with soil, and creates the raw materials from which new rocks are born.

Most erosion takes time, and lots of it. While a strong downpour in the desert or an unexpected cloudburst over a rain-soaked forest can cause massive and sudden erosion, it usually takes hundreds, thousands, or even millions of years to significantly change

Water, from rain, from snow, constantly erodes the Minaret Mountains in Inyo National Forest, California. Water is a powerful force in shaping the earth.

a landscape. Every thousand years, 3.3 inches (8.4 cm) of our planet's rocky surface wears away and turns to soil or sand. Imagine, then, how long it took for the Appalachian Mountains to erode to their current height! They once stood at least 31,680 feet (9,656 m) tall, but the tallest peak in the Appalachians today is Mount Mitchell, in North Carolina, at 6,684 feet (2,037 m) above sea level.

Our world is filled with natural forces that cause erosion. Water carves channels into solid rock, creating wonders like the Grand Canyon. Glaciers inch along, tearing off small chunks of stone as they polish and shape mountainsides. Waves beat against a coastal shoreline, breaking off pieces of cliffs. Wind blows sand across the desert, carving the rocks it touches. And people contribute to the process by cutting forests, digging ditches, and building roads—activities that loosen soil to be carried away by wind and water. Erosion is a monumental force on our planet. We can't prevent it from happening, but we can learn how to minimize our impact on the earth to keep our lush forests and farmlands growing into the future.

Mount Mitchell is not very high, as mountains go. But it's old enough to have eroded to one fifth its former height.

To shape landscapes, erosion needs some helping hands—weathering and deposition. While weathering changes the characteristics of rocks in place, erosion loosens and carries away material. Without weathering, erosion wouldn't be very effective. Deposition happens when eroded materials pile up in a new place. Together, these partners can move mountains!

MECHANICAL WEATHERING

Waves crash against a sandy beach. A hard rain falls on a rocky hilltop, sending water running down its sides in a mad rush. A tiny pool of water inside a cracked rock freezes. Wind carries clouds of dust across a plain. All of these forces—one object striking another—cause mechanical weathering, allowing the weakened rocks to erode.

ROOT CAUSES. By tapping their root systems into the ground, plants contribute to the slow and inevitable breakup of rocks. Grasses wedge their roots into tiny crevices in small rocks, causing fractures. Trees cling to hillsides, driving their roots like drills through faults in rocky surfaces. As tree, shrub, and grass roots grow, they push deeper into the rock, creating cracks where there was once solid rock. Soon, the rock breaks into pieces.

CRACKING UP. Ice is the power blaster of all weathering forces. Water seeps into tiny crevices in rocks. When it freezes, it pushes against the sides of a crevice with a force equal to the weight of a mile-high ice cube! Unable to resist, the rock splits, shattering. This process happens over and over again, breaking entire mountainsides into pebbles that are carried off in mountain streams.

Wide swings in temperature also make rocks crack. In the desert, it might be 100°F (38°C) in the sunshine at noon, and 40°F (4°C) in the chill of the night. During the

Trees play a part in the continuous process of erosion.

heat of the day, rocks soak up the sunlight and expand a little. At night, as they chill down, they contract. This tiny bit of movement encourages cracks to spread a little further every day. The outer layers of the rock may peel off like an onion skin! It doesn't take a desert to make a rock peel, however—just constant variations between daytime and nighttime temperatures. Layers of Half Dome, in Yosemite National Park, California, constantly peel off and fall to the valley below. The mountain of Corcovado, towering over the harbor of Rio de Janeiro, Brazil, also shows this crazy onionskin weathering.

CHEMICAL WEATHERING

Cool, dry climates rely on temperature extremes to trigger mechanical weathering. But in warm or damp places with deep forests, like the rain forests of Papua New Guinea, another process comes into play—chemical weathering.

THE ACID TEST. Chemical weathering changes rocks on an atomic level. By adding chemicals to existing rocks, it rearranges the atoms in a rock to make it more prone to erosion. And the chief agent of chemical weathering is rain.

If you can find an old graveyard, look at the oldest headstones. Sometimes the stone is so eroded you can hardly read the name. Sure enough, raindrops are to blame! Rainwater is slightly acidic, so it eats away at the surface of stones. When airborne sulfur dioxide (from the burning of fossil fuels in cars, trucks, and buses) mixes with rainwater, it creates acid rain—a much more potent acid. Acid rain quickly erodes soft rocks, like limestone, and also causes harder rocks like granite and basalt (used for headstones) to erode.

As rain seeps into the ground it flows through humus-laden soil and layers of decaying leaves, picking up carbonic acid—the same acid that puts the bubbles in your soda pop. This mild acid eats away at soft rocks, widening cracks in the bedrock and etching new pathways deep under the earth's surface.

SHAPE SHIFTING

Weathering along fractures in rocks creates almost perfectly round boulders, rocks, and pebbles. Weathering in crevices will gradually deepen the crevices, as in the grooved granite boulders found throughout Acadia National Park in Maine. But weathering is a very uneven process. It's rare to see a cliff break apart in pieces all the same size. The breakdown depends entirely on the type of rock that is being attacked. Some rocks, like lime-stone, have very regular cracks and crevices, and they break apart easily. Others, like granite, have few cracks in them, and weathering takes a lot of time. As these forces attack a cliff, they wear down the soft sedimentary rocks first. Metamorphic rock wears down a little more slowly. And igneous rock wears down very, very slowly.

When multiple types of rock are mixed together in a single place, erosion and weathering will ensure that the softest rocks disappear first. When different types of rock are mixed in a single cliff face, this creates some strange landscapes. The Garden of the Gods, in Colorado, is a collec-tion of oddly shaped towers of hard rock left behind when the softer rocks eroded. The Great Stone Face of New Hampshire is a cliff that eroded into a giant face! And Natural Bridge, in Virginia, is a sweeping arc of stone spanning a gap of 100 feet (30 m), hovering 165 feet (50 m) above a small creek. Cavern collapse and stream erosion joined forces to create this massive monument.

Natural Bridge in Virginia

RECYCLING ROCKS

When erosion carries away materials, it has to drop them somewhere. This process is called deposition. Wind deposits sand into dunes, sculpted hills that shift every time the wind blows. Waves pile up sand into beaches along the coastline. Glaciers leave behind vast hills of drift, the rocky material they carry within their icy grip. Streams deposit silt and other sediments along their banks, leaving behind rich soil when they flood. Deltas form where rivers spill vast plains of sediment into the sea. These deposited sediments gradually solidify into mudstone or sandstone, creating new sedimentary rocks. Together, erosion and deposition form a never-ending process by which the rock and mineral components of the earth are recycled.

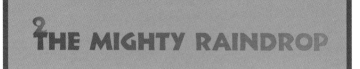

On an 1869 expedition to map the Colorado River, geologist John Wesley Powell discovered a fairyland of rock formations. In a report to Washington, D.C., he wrote : "Wherever we look there is but a wilderness of rocks—deep gorges where the rivers are lost below cliffs and towers and pinnacles, and ten thousand strangely carved forms in every direction."

In the Colorado River basin, Arizona, New Mexico, and Utah contain some of the world's most unusual rock formations. The Colorado River winds through the Grand Canyon, cutting a channel that is now more than a mile deep. Sharp needles and soaring pinnacles of stone rise from Bryce Canyon, Utah. Gigantic wind-polished curved arches dominate the landscape in Arches National Park, Utah. Water and wind roar through the strangely curved shapes of the slot canyons in Canyonlands National Park, Utah.

And it all started with a raindrop.

Every time a drop of water splashes on something, it causes a little bit of erosion. You may not notice it happening on such a small scale. But not only does the acid in a raindrop eat into rock, a raindrop pounds on the ground with a significant amount of force.

Marble Canyon, Arizona, was a separate park until the boundaries of Grand Canyon National Park were extended up the Colorado River to include it.

Imagine billions of raindrops banging the ground like tiny hammers, each knocking a single tiny particle into the air. As each particle bounces away, it heads downhill, pulled by the force of gravity. A particle may not travel very far on each bounce. But after billions and billions of raindrops push it around, who knows where it will end up?

Every raindrop plays a part in the ongoing saga of erosion. During a rainstorm, water flows downhill in sheets. As these sheets of water move across the ground, they carry away loose particles of soil. The water collects in any eroded spots on the ground. If the water accumulates in a pool and stays there, we call it a puddle. But if a tiny path erodes for the water to keep flowing downhill, that path is called a rill. Water running through rills continues to cut into the soil, scooping out more particles and widening the path. Eventually, the eroded pathway becomes deep enough to be called a gully. Gullies may drain into streams, ponds, lakes, or swamps—anywhere where water collects in large quantities.

As rainwater seeps into the ground, it runs along natural slopes in the bedrock, gradually widening and enlarging the existing joints—natural cracks between layers of rock. Weathering takes over when water freezes in joints, making the rocks shatter. Running water—streams and rivers—carry particles of rocks and sand, scrubbing at the bedrock. So eventually, the softer bedrock wears away, leaving the harder rock behind as pinnacles, needles, and arches.

MAKOSCHE SHICA

Layers of mud and sandstone make up the Badlands of South Dakota, where rainfall carves amazing shapes. Because of the rugged stone peaks, the Sioux called the area *makosche shica*—"bad land"—and the French trappers they befriended called the place *mauvaises terres à*

Gullies eroded in sandstone in Badlands National Park, South Dakota

traverser, or "bad lands to cross." There are no streams in the Badlands. Rain-fed gullies cut deep into the sandstone and mud, creating pyramids, knobs, and hoodoos—tall columns of rock.

INSTANT EROSION

Sometimes a heavy rainfall doesn't soak into the ground quickly enough. Water races down steep hillsides, carrying along loose particles and small rocks. The effects can be devastating. Water

Devils Tower, Wyoming, is the core of a volcano, left behind as the mountain washed away.

RAIN FOREST "VITAMINS"

In Peru, along the Tambopata River at Quechua, the daily rainfall of the Amazon rain forest erodes a large red clay cliff, 164 feet (50 m) high and 1,641 feet (500 m) long, creating the biggest clay slick in the world! Tapirs, capybara, howler monkeys, pigeons, and parrots gather at the crumbling cliff. Brilliant blue and gold macaws flock by the hundreds to the slippery clay banks and peck at the mud. Why? The eroded clay provides essential minerals—a dose of rain forest vitamins—that lets these animals neutralize the toxic effects of some of the fruits and seeds they normally eat.

Scarlet macaws and red and green macaws flock to lick mineral-rich clay in Manu National Park, Peru.

accumulates in every low spot, flooding valleys and overwhelming streams. Rivers jump their banks, carrying off boats and washing away homes. These flash floods cause instant erosion, tearing away vast chunks of soil as they accelerate downhill.

In the desert, rainfall from a sudden cloudburst cuts deeply into the soft clay and sand. Dry washes fill with raging streams. Since there is so little vegetation in the desert, there is nothing to anchor the soil. Runoff from a downburst causes widespread erosion, where the water cuts deep channels called dry washes into the desert floor. Once the water vanishes, the dry washes provide newfound shade for plants and animals.

Gradual erosion from rainfall creates beautiful landforms in deserts. Inselbergs (German for "island mountain") look like sharp, steep needles of rock rising from the desert floor. Buttes—extremely tall, steep pinnacles—remain behind as temporary streams cut deeper and deeper into the original desert floor. And mesas (Spanish for "table") are wide, flat plateaus where hard, water-resistant layers of lava protect the underlying softer bedrock.

The rainfall of the Amazon rain forest, gushing through thousands of tributaries, contributes a great deal to the world's largest river. The Amazon River pumps more than eight trillion gallons (30 trillion liters) of water a day into the Atlantic Ocean! Its water flow is greater than the next eight largest rivers in the world—combined.

CARVING UNDERGROUND WORLDS

In regions where the underlying rock is soft, rainwater performs slow and steady erosion underground. Carrying along carbonic acid, or calcium carbonate, the water drips through tiny openings (called pores) in the rock. It widens joints and creates larger and larger gaps. Eventually, the slow trickle of water into the ground carves out caverns at the water table, the elevation at which the water surface settles underground. If the water table drops, water will flow downward, creating underground streams that more fiercely erode the bedrock. As the water table drops further, these tunnels slowly fill with air—and deposition begins.

Deposition of calcite (and certain other minerals) carried away by erosion creates the wonderland we associate with caverns. Water dripping through a crack creates stalactites (pointing down) and stalagmites (pointing up). When water slowly trickles in sheets through caverns, it leaves behind larger formations, such as flowstone, draperies, and shields. There are many other types of deposits in a cavern, from cave pearls to helictites—at least forty different types of formations!

Caverns created by water erosion form in karst, bedrock that includes all rocks that dissolve easily when exposed to natural

ETCHED IN STONE

Calcium carbonate isn't the only acid that can carve a cavern. In New Mexico, the vast Lechuguilla Cave—1,565 feet (477 m) deep—is thought to have formed from hydrogen sulfide gases bubbling up through the limestone, eroding the cave from the bottom up! Another cavern in Mexico proves that this deadly gas, rising from deep volcanic activity, still creates caves today. Wearing gas masks and special environmental suits, explorers entered Cueva de Villa Luz and found strange new microbes and insects thriving in deadly acids. Stalactites teeming with life, called "snottites," constantly drip gobs of these acid-loving creatures onto the cavern floor! The explorers likened the lively environment to the sulfuric bubbling of a black smoker on the bottom of the ocean floor.

Snottites are gooey stalactites of microscopic gypsum crystals covered in bacteria. They thrive in an extremely acidic environment.

acids. Limestone is the most common type of karst, but caverns also form in other types of karst, like gypsum and chalk. But erosion in karst doesn't just happen underground. On the surface, limestone clearly shows etching by acidic rainwater. On a miniature scale, raindrops widen joints and wear down soft rock, creating ridges, grooves, and tiny holes. Weakened surface rock may cause a cavern roof to suddenly collapse, making a sinkhole. Or erosion may leave a cap of cavern roof behind as the rest of the cavern walls erode, forming a natural bridge.

Mighty raindrops dig channels, erode caverns, and shape pinnacles. No matter how much water is involved—a single drop, a bucketful, or a raging river—water acts like a sculptor's tool, carving and etching the earth's surface.

THE DITCH DIGGER

When water is on the run, it can do much more than carve caverns—it can move mountains! Given time, running water cuts channels many thousands of feet deep into stone, digging huge ditches. One of the world's deepest canyons, the Colca River Canyon of Peru, dwarfs the Grand Canyon in depth. The Colca is nearly 2 miles (3 km) deep, deep enough that the trip to the bottom is like hiking to the bottom of the Grand Canyon—and climbing most of the way back out.

Running water shapes mountain landscapes. The water may pool from rainfall, or flow from trickling springs. Collecting in rills, the water follows gravity, scooping out soil and soft rock to make a regular path. Once the path supports a constant flow of water, a stream is born.

Dropping from high elevations, these young streams cut steep, V-shaped valleys. They create water gaps, making a trail for others to follow. During the westward expansion of the United States, settlers followed rivers and looked for water gaps to show them the way through the Appalachian Mountains. The Delaware Water Gap is one such showy site, where the Delaware River eroded through a tight spot in tilted layers of hard rock.

As the stream works its way through a tight passage, the velocity of the water increases. This creates more friction against

Colca Canyon in Peru is nearly twice as deep as the Grand Canyon.

the underlying rock. By eroding mineral fragments and sand from the rocks, the stream builds up a stream load—a suspension load of suspended debris and a bedload of larger grains that roll and slide along the bottom. Together they do the dirty work of erosion. Like sandpaper, the stream load scrubs against the stream walls, carving away more loose material. It polishes the harder rocks, making smooth, slippery surfaces. Streams running at high velocities carry a heavy stream load. As the stream slows

POTHOLES

Potholes occur when some of the stream load gets trapped in a circular current, an eddy, spinning around and around like a washing machine. Eventually, it carves a rounded hole in the rocky bottom of the stream. In 1884 a group of Pennsylvania coal miners discovered Archibald Pothole. It's the world's largest pothole— 38 feet (12 m) deep and 42 feet (13 m) wide across the top.

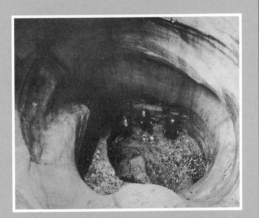

The Archibald Pothole in Archibald, Pennsylvania, is the largest in the world. When discovered, the pothole was still partly full of the rounded stones that helped to erode it.

down, this debris settles, filling the streambed. The lightest particles— mineral-rich silt, clay, and sand—stay suspended for the ride to the sea.

While the stream load does most of the erosion, carbonic acid in the water also helps etch away bits of stone. And in bouncing, bubbly streams, the explosion of bubbles that hit each rocky surface has an impact of several thousand pounds per square inch.

WHEN WATER FALLS

From roaring rapids to plunging cataracts, water tends to fall downhill. Waterfalls occur anywhere the stream bottom suddenly changes from harder rock to softer rock. When a waterfall drops over a ledge, the stream load cuts away strongly at the resistant rock face. Eventually, the rock erodes, and the waterfall seems to "walk" backward! The waterfall's contribution to erosion becomes its downfall as it disintegrates from a mighty cascade into a series of low rapids.

The Niagara River provides an excellent example of a waterfall's erosive action. Queenston, Ontario, is where the falls used to be, 12,300 years ago and 7.1 miles (11.4 km) downstream. As the waterfall "walked" backward, it carved the Niagara Gorge, which is up to 300 feet (91 m) deep in places. Each year, the Horseshoe Falls continues to move back 5 feet (1.5 m). The American Falls erodes more slowly, at a rate of 6 inches (15 cm)

This view from Horseshoe Falls, the Canadian side of Niagara Falls, lets you see how the falls is working its way upstream.

per year. Niagara Falls will continue moving upriver until it reaches Lake Erie, 8,000 years from now—unless it turns into rapids on its way upstream.

The force of the water landing at the bottom of a waterfall quickly erodes the rock below, creating a deep plunge pool. The plunge pool at the base of Horseshoe Falls is more than 184 feet (56 m) deep.

FINISHING THE RACE

Streams slow down as the land around them flattens out. While the words *river* and *stream* are geologically interchangeable, we tend to think of water flowing through a wide valley as a river. Rivers on flat plains do most of their erosion from side to side. Currents cut mud and rocks away from the outside of curves and deposit debris on the inside of curves. As the valley widens, it defines the river's floodplain—the area where the river has previ-

FLOODS AND FARMING

The country of Bangladesh sits on lowlands and deltas formed by rivers draining India and the Himalaya Mountains. It's the eastern part of the world's largest delta, the Ganges-Brahmaputra Delta, 300 miles (483 km) long and 100 miles

A lack of flooding is now the big problem in the Nile Delta. For thousands of years, the Egyptians relied on seasonal Nile River floods to provide rich farmland in a desert region. When they built the Aswan High Dam in 1964, the Egyptians gained electrical power—but

Flooding in Bangladesh is an annual event. The people who live there weigh the risk of the floods against the benefits of fertile farmland.

(161 km) wide. At least a fifth of Bangladesh disappears under floodwaters every year. Despite the difficulty of living on ever-shifting islands, people remain there because they can farm. Flooding adds more than 2 billion tons of fertile soil to the plains and deltas of Bangladesh every year.

they lost their natural floods. Their farmland is vanishing. And without new sediment to build it up, the land around the Nile Delta is slowly sinking into the Mediterranean Sea. By the year 2100, the Egyptian coastline will move inland enough to force more than a million people to migrate to higher ground.

ously left deposits. These lowlands mark the extent to which the river, over time, has eroded into the surrounding landscape.

As the river becomes older, the region between the streams that feed it wears down closer and closer to sea level—the ultimate level that running water seeks out. It may meander back and forth like a snake, even cutting itself off in places.

Eventually, all streams have to deposit their stream load. When a stream tumbles out of a mountain area into a flat plain, it suddenly slows down. The stream load is deposited, forming an alluvial fan or alluvial cone. There is a large alluvial cone near the base of Mount Shasta, California. But a more common deposit is a delta, created where the stream flows into another body of water. This triangular-shaped fan of silt and sediment gradually builds new land, providing farmers with mineral-rich soil. Sediments may also wash out to sea. The Mississippi River drops more than a quarter of a billion tons of sediment into the Gulf of Mexico every year.

A RIVER REVIVED

Sometimes, a mature river springs back to life. It behaves like a young stream again, eroding downward into the surrounding plain. This can occur if the sea level at the river's mouth drops, or a change in climate adds rainfall into its flow. Or the land around a river, undergoing mountain-building processes, may lift up into the air, giving the river another chance at carving downhill.

A rejuvenated river cuts into its new plateau, carrying away the least resistant rock. It leaves behind terraces of stone to mark its passage. As the river continues to cut down into the rock below it, these terraces—left stranded on cliffs—show where the water level used to be.

Eroding its way deep down, the river meanders then cuts into bedrock. It can create a steep-sided gorge or a winding canyon. Many of the world's deepest canyons—the Colca in Peru, the Grand Canyon, and the 3-mile (4.8-km)-deep Himalayan gorges of the Ganges River—are carved into lands uplifted during mountain building.

27

4 WAVE-WASHED SHORES

From the islands of the South Pacific to the rocky coves of Lake Superior, waves beat against shorelines, causing constant erosion. When waves pound against a cliff, the water exerts a tremendous force against the rocks. During the split second that a wave pushes against a cliff, the air in the cracks and crevices in the rock gets compressed. Having nowhere else to go, the air expands and shatters the rock. This pressure—2,500 pounds per square foot (10 tons per square meter)—acts like a jackhammer, breaking the rock further with each crash of a wave. During a storm, the force may be even greater. A storm wave 18 feet (5.5 m) tall can pick up and throw a 10-ton boulder.

Waves also use sand and loose rock to sculpt the shoreline. And salt water itself can eat into soft rocks like limestone. Between the slamming force behind the waves, the abrading debris they carry, and the corrosive action of salt water, coastal cliffs erode at a rate of 3 feet (1 m) or more each year.

At the base of a cliff, waves first create a terrace, a bench of rock at the height of the high-tide waves. Small stones and pebbles, acting as cutting tools, may scrub away at the top of the terrace and form a pothole, much like those found in mountain

This is part of a formation of sea stacks known as the Twelve Apostles, off the southern Australia coast.

streams. If seawater sloshes into the pothole and stays there, it may become a tidal pool, soon teeming with life.

Attacking the lower reaches of the cliff, the waves carve into the softest rock. Just like the erosive action of rainwater, seawater soaks into the pores of the rock. It cuts away at the fractures and joints, widening and deepening them. Blocks of rock fall away from the cliff face, undercutting the top of the cliff. Soon, the cliff may hang over the sea. Once undercut deeply enough, the top of the cliff will crash down to the shore.

Headlands—cliffs that stick far out into the sea—are the coastal cliffs most prone to erosion. Since waves can crash against both sides of a headland, it erodes twice as fast as a regular cliff. The waves hollow out crevices, forming a sea cave. Sea caves are often shallow, but some are very deep. Fingal's Cave, in Scotland, is a deep sea cave carved into basalt pillars. Islands with limestone cliffs tend to have many sea caves. One Greek island, Paxos, has more than forty sea caves in only 3 miles (4.8 km) of shoreline.

Crashing into the inner walls of a sea cave, waves may continue their erosion upward and create a spouting horn, or a blowhole. Some of the sea caves in small islands off Vancouver Island have blowholes, as does one in the Galápagos Islands. Just like the jet of water from a whale spout, a blowhole erupts like a geyser when a wave sprays out through the opening.

The waves may break through the headland, knocking the back wall out of the sea cave to create a sea arch. If the arch collapses, it may leave behind a pillar of harder rock—a sea stack. Waves continue to erode the base of a sea stack, giving it a shape like a giant vase. Eventually it, too, will collapse into the sea.

BUILDING NEW COASTLINE

What waves take away from one place, they give to another. Carried by currents that sweep along every coastline, eroded material ends up deposited as a beach. The beach may be a sweeping expanse of sand, a collection of wave-rounded rocks, or a deep layer of polished gravel. It all depends on what raw materials were carried and sorted by the waves.

Most beaches extend 30 feet (9 m) into the water, disappearing below the waterline of the lowest tide. Waves sort their deposits by size, pushing the tiniest fragments the farthest up the beach and creating layers of larger and larger material that retreat beneath the sea. The ripple marks on a sandy beach form as waves push more sand toward the shore. As the water runs back off, the current pushes grains of sand back into the water—a constant tug of war between erosion and deposition.

Sandbars—small islands of sand forming in the shallows off the coastline—build up from the material that either erodes from nearby headlands or is carried from the existing beaches into the shallows by a strong current. A sand spit is an extension of the beach, sticking out into the water like a small peninsula. Sometimes it curves back on itself like a hook, like Sandy Hook south of New York's harbor. Sandbars and sand spits often appear only during low tide. Sometimes a sandbar or sand spit can build up enough to cut off the tide, trapping seawater in a lagoon.

Beaches are constantly on the move. Sand sweeps back into the water with every wave and may be deposited slightly up the beach seconds later on the next wave. To prevent the constant movement of beaches, some communities build barriers—jetties—to trap sand as it moves away from their beach. But a jetty can

COLORFUL BEACHES

While we tend to think of white or yellow sand beaches, beaches occur in a variety of colors. In the Caribbean Sea, coral reefs and seashells erode to provide material for island beaches. Many of the Caribbean islands have brilliant white sand beaches, but the beaches of Bermuda are soft pink. Black sand beaches result from eroded basalt, as along the coastline of Oregon, or from eroded volcanic debris, like the black sand beaches of Hawaii, Montserrat, and Martinique.

Most black sand beach photographs you'll see are of Hawaiian beaches, but black sand is created by wave action wherever there is basalt at the coastline. This beach is in Iceland.

cause more harm than good by disrupting the natural patterns of the waves. The plan sometimes backfires, since currents near a jetty may start to scoop even more sand off the beach, accelerating erosion to the point that the "protected" beach disappears.

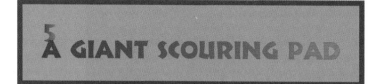
5
A GIANT SCOURING PAD

Seven times in the earth's long history, swarms of glaciers flowed from high mountains and polar regions, creating a blanket of slow-moving ice. The weight and friction of these rivers of ice eroded the earth dramatically. Like a gigantic scouring pad, a glacier can smooth jagged rocky surfaces to a smooth polish, carving breathtaking landscapes through mountain ranges.

The last ice age ended almost 10,000 years ago. At its peak, ice covered more than 30 percent of the earth's surface. These glaciers carved out and carried rocks and soil over vast distances. As the earth warmed up and the glaciers retreated, melting, they left their loads of rocks, gravel, water, and soil behind.

The ice-age glaciers contributed significantly to shaping the landscapes we know today. But glaciers still cover 10 percent of our planet, another active element in the earth's erosion process.

Forming either at high latitudes or high altitudes, a glacier starts out as a massive snowpack, 100 feet (30 m) thick or more. As newer snow buries older snow, the older snow gets crushed into a thick block of tightly interlocked ice crystals. This unusually thick ice eventually starts to move like a glob of melted plastic. It flows downhill very slowly, carrying the snowpack along for the ride.

Moreno Glacier in Los Glaciares National Park, Peru

Glacial ice moves like a bulldozer, scraping rocks clean. More effective at erosion than a river or a stream, a glacier carries a massive amount of debris along inside the ice. The debris helps the glacier cut channels through soft mountainsides and scratch deep grooves in hard rocks. And the thicker the ice, the better the glacier is at erosion, which is why the glaciers of the ice ages did such a good job at carving into mountains. In New Hampshire, deep grooves in the White Mountains—granite peaks 6,000 feet (1,829 m) tall—indicate that parts of the state were once under a glacier at least 8,000 feet (2,438 m) thick.

But as the glacier's thick ice scrapes against rocky walls, it also contributes to the reduction of the glacier. By creating friction inside the glacial ice, the ice starts to move at different speeds. The sides slow down, and the center moves more quickly. The hard-packed snow on top begins to crack, creating crevasses up to 200 feet (61 m) deep. Water—from melting snow and occasional rain-storms—flows into the crevasses, creating streams within the ice. This erodes the inside of the glacier. Its movement becomes erratic. If enough melting affects the glacier's face, it will start to retreat. It doesn't actually move uphill, but it looks like it does because it is melting. The face of a melting glacier shows the thick ice inside glowing an unusual "icy" blue.

TYPES OF GLACIERS

Glaciers that begin on high mountaintops and flow into valleys between mountains are called valley glaciers. A valley glacier moves about 656 feet (200 m) each year. As the glacier moves through a valley, it turns the V-shaped notch carved by a stream into a U-shaped valley that looks like a giant ditch. Glacial valleys are usually long and straight, with gentle lower slopes that rise up to steep mountainsides. Yosemite Valley in California is a glacial valley. If the glacial valley forms at a high elevation, it may abruptly drop off the edge of a mountain or plateau as a hanging valley. Hanging valleys often contain spectacular waterfalls, such as the Bridal Veil Fall in Yosemite National Park. It drops 620 feet (189 m).

Valley glaciers scoop out soft rock from the valley floor and carry it along. When the glacier retreats, water may flow into these depressions and create small lakes that look like a string of beads from the air. Or the entire valley may fill up to create a deep glacial lake.

When a glacier reaches the sea, it is called an outlet glacier. These glaciers, often 100 feet (30 m) high, constantly drop, or "calve," icebergs into the sea. The narrow valleys created by outlet glaciers become fjords. Fjords define the rugged coastline of

A calving glacier in Alaska: To see glaciers calve, you can take a boat trip along coastlines with glaciers.

Norway. These deep channels are up to 120 miles (193 km) long and 4,000 feet (1,219 m) deep. Fjords are also found in New Zealand, Alaska, Canada, Patagonia, and Iceland. The world's deepest fjord, in southern Chile, is 4,226 feet (1,288 m) deep.

During the ice ages, continental glaciers—also known as ice caps, or ice sheets—covered many parts of the earth. Ice once covered the pampas of Argentina and spread across New South Wales and Tasmania, Australia, and New Zealand. In spite of their current warm climates, Turkey, Syria, and Iran were once blanketed by glaciers. Even the Pacific Islands of New Guinea and Formosa show the effects of glaciers. But today, Greenland and Antarctica are the primary places on earth covered by continental glaciers. The glaciers of Greenland may drop as much as 50 cubic miles (80 cubic km) of ice into the North Atlantic every year.

During the ice ages, continental glaciers carved deeply into the lowlands as well. Digging through weak bedrock, they created the Great Lakes—Lake Michigan, Lake Superior, Lake Huron, Lake Erie, and Lake Ontario—which straddle the border between the United States and Canada. Lake Superior, with 31,820 square miles (82,414 sq km) of water, is the world's largest freshwater surface. Always windswept, its waves can grow large enough to capsize a large freighter. Its shoreline has sea caves and arches in high cliffs, sand dunes, and more than 1,000 miles (1,609 km) of beaches covered with wave-rounded stones.

BURIED IN ICE

A remnant of the last ice age, the ice cap on Greenland once covered much of northern Europe, northern Asia, and eastern Canada. It buried the northern and eastern United States in ice, stretching south into northern New Jersey and west to St. Louis, Missouri. The enormous weight of this ice cap—more than 2 miles (3.2 km) thick in places—crushes the land underneath it. If the ice cap over Greenland melted tomorrow, the world's oceans would rise by 25 feet (7.6 m). And there is enough glacial ice piled up over Antarctica to bury the entire United States 9,000 feet (2,743 m) deep in ice.

GRINDING THROUGH ROCK

If you've ever used a rock tumbler, you may be familiar with how rough, dull rocks can be turned into glistening, polished stones. A glacier uses the same tools as a rock tumbler to polish stones and smooth the sides of mountains.

GLACIAL SCULPTURES

As glaciers erode mountains, they leave behind unique formations. When a glacier starts working its way down a mountain, the expansion and contraction of its ice at the top carves a cirque. These depressions look like a big scoop out of solid rock. After the glacier is gone, a cirque may develop a glacial lake, reflecting the skies with a mirrorlike surface. Perched in the Sierra Nevada, Tulainyo Lake, 12,802 feet (3,902 m) above sea level, is the highest lake in the United States, filling an ancient cirque.

When two glaciers descend down opposite sides of the same mountain, they carve an arête. This mountain ridge has jagged, thin rock walls that look like the blade of a steak knife pointing toward the sky. Parts of the Garden Wall, an arête along the Continental Divide in Glacier National Park, are so thin at the top that the sun can shine through it. And if three glaciers descend down the same mountain peak, they create a matterhorn. Named for the spectacular Matterhorn in the Swiss Alps, the peak resembles a sharply pointed pyramid.

Weathered rock fractures under the weight of a glacier. As the glacier flows down a mountainside, it may cleanly break the rock layers beneath it. Once the glacier retreats, the gigantic steps it created in this process are called a riegel, or giant's stairway.

Milky streams, colored by a type of silt called rock flour, pour off the leading edge of a receding glacier. Mount Rainier, in Washington, has many of

The Garden Wall (left) in Glacier National Park, Montana, is an example of an arête, while Mount Oberlin (center) is a matterhorn.

these streams flowing down its sides, carrying fine silt and gravel to the base of the mountain. When the water from these streams flows into a lake, the suspended particles of rock flour make the water turn a vivid turquoise. Lake Louise, in Banff National Park (Alberta, Canada), and Grinnell Lake in Glacier National Park (Montana), are just two of thousands of these beautiful mountain lakes colored by glacial sediments.

Sometimes a retreating glacier will leave a big chunk of ice behind. The ice will melt and erode the ground under it, creating a kettle lake. A kettle lake can also form underneath a retreating glacier from the sheer force of melting water pouring out of the ice.

Ice itself isn't much of a sculpting agent. The weight and pressure of the sides of a glacier can break chunks of rock off a mountainside, but it takes more subtle means to carve lasting impressions in the rock. Just like a stream, a glacier relies on its load of debris to do most of the work. Like the "rough grit" of a rock tumbler, these rocks get carried along inside the glacial ice. As these rough surfaces scrub against the sides of a valley, they cut scratches and grooves into the existing rock and break off other rough pieces for the glacier to carry along. They also grind off bits of rock into rock flour. In turn, the debris erodes. This "smooth grit" can't break rocks off the sides of the valley, but it can scrub them like fine sandpaper. The smallest bits of debris—especially rock flour—act like the final stage of polish in a rock tumbler. They rub against rough rocks, making them smooth and shiny.

All of this loose material accumulates in patterns, called moraines, inside the glacier. Lateral moraines form like dirty ribbons along the sides of the glacier, where most of the erosion is going on. As rocks and gravel tumble onto the glacier from the sides of the valley, they slowly sink into the ice. Some of them get left behind in long, thin bands. If two glaciers meet, their lateral moraines merge, creating a medial moraine.

HILLS OF TILL

As a glacier recedes, it dumps its load of drift (eroded material) and everything else it has carried along for the ride. A retreating glacier frequently leaves behind a series of long, low hills full of till—a random mix of sand, clay, silt, rocks, and boulders. These till-filled hills are called terminal moraines. Cape Cod, Massachusetts, and Long Island, New York, both built up around terminal moraines left during the last ice age.

As the ice melts, the remaining till gets carried along by the water and accumulates into small hills. Kames are cone-shaped hills left behind by a glacier's retreat. Eskers are long, thin hills up to 30 feet (9 m) wide and almost as tall. These winding ridges can stretch on for miles. An esker develops as sand and gravel deposits build up in layers, left behind by streams running

39

GRASSHOPPERS ON ICE

Sometimes a glacier picks up more than just rocks. Dark black ribbons of frozen grasshoppers decorate Grasshopper Glacier in Montana, near the northeast entrance to Yellowstone National Park. You can hike up to the glacier and see the grasshoppers, buried 60 feet (18 m) deep.

through or under the glacier. A drumlin forms in a teardrop shape, with the pointy end facing the direction of the glacier's retreat. In a drumlin, the till is tightly packed. There are thousands of drumlins, found in groups, scattered across Wisconsin, Minnesota, New England, Nova Scotia, and Finland. Both Beacon Hill and Bunker Hill in Boston are drumlins.

Glaciers also leave behind giant boulders, called erratics. Carried as far as 750 miles (1,207 km), these out-of-place boulders are made of different types of rock than the bedrock surrounding them. One slab of glacially transported limestone left in Warren County, Ohio, weighs more than 13,500 tons. Erratics pepper the landscape across Canada and the northern United States. Glaciers dropped off significant minerals as well. Diamonds from the Canadian northwest made it to the streams of Montana. Glaciers even carried native copper from the Upper Peninsula of Michigan and dropped little chunks of it across Iowa, Illinois, and Ohio.

Most important, glacial soils left behind create rich farmland— if there aren't too many big rocks in the mix. Because glaciers do such a good job of grinding rocks into rock flour, the soil is loaded with the mineral nutrients that plants need. The "breadbasket" farming regions of the midwestern United States and Canada are based on glacial soils.

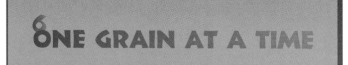

6 ONE GRAIN AT A TIME

Howling winds carry tiny particles. One grain at a time, these agents of erosion pummel against existing rocks, smoothing and polishing their edges, abrading and removing rough material.

Sand is a powerful cutting force. Painters use sandblasting equipment—an application of erosion to technology—to remove dirt and graffiti from stone walls. But sand isn't the only particle to aid in wind erosion. Volcanic ash—fine, dustlike particles thrown high into the atmosphere by volcanoes—can also serve as a cutting tool, as can flakes of gypsum and grains of dust, silt, and salt. No matter whether the wind is moving across the Sahara Desert or over a parking lot at the mall, it's carrying plenty of ammunition for erosion.

The tiniest particles—silt, dust, and ash—are light enough to be lifted and carried by the wind. Dust from Australia travels more than 1,400 miles (2,253 km) and lands on New Zealand. Japan gets showered by dust carried 1,000 miles (1,609 km) or more from China. But most particles just bounce along. They rise, kicked up by the wind, and fall down again, pushing themselves or another particle or two up into the wind. Like tiny bouncing balls, they move along very close to the ground.

While this satellite photograph doesn't let you see specific rock formations in the Tibesti Mountains, it clearly shows the winds that begin in
the Libyan Desert and blow into Chad. The Tibesti Mountains, of volcanic origin, are the dark area at right, while the Ennendi Plateau is a
sandstone formation at left–a duststorm is raging in the desert between
the two. Wind erosion is a force with an enormous range.

Wind erosion includes two very different forces, deflation and abrasion. Deflation occurs where there is no vegetation to protect the ground. The wind picks up and removes particles from the ground. As the fine particles drift off, only the heavier particles remain. Eventually, all that is left on the ground are the particles and rocks that are too heavy for the wind to move. The ground becomes a desert pavement, a rough cobblestone-like surface of rocks worn smooth by the scouring action of wind-borne sand.

Abrasion is a natural form of sandblasting. Fine sand particles suspended in the wind abrade, or rub against, the surfaces they hit. Some rocks, like granite, become pitted. Others, like quartzite, take on a fine polish. Solid surfaces are etched by the particles in the wind, so the surface of a rock begins to look like lace. Rocky zeugens, formed by abrasion, look like the deeply eroded limestone pavements created by rainfall. But their jagged edges come from the constant pounding of grains of sand against soft rock.

SCULPTED BY THE WIND

When the wind erodes a hollow, creating a valley, it's called a blowout. Blowouts can be as deep as the water table, and hundreds of miles long. The wind carves blowouts in poor soil and in sand dunes. But it can also scour a blowout into solid granite, such as those formed in the Gobi Desert. North Africa, Mongolia, and Turkey all contain significant blowout regions.

Pedestals, also known as hoodoos, prove that most wind erosion occurs close to the ground. As grains of sand bounce along in the wind, they reach a maximum height of about 3 feet (1 m). The sand strikes the pedestal, knocks out a grain or two, and keeps going. Eventually, what was once a tall slender pillar of stone is now shaped like a mushroom—with a thin pillar at the bottom and a thick cap at least 3 feet in the air.

Ventifacts are desert boulders that have been shaped by the wind. One side of the boulder looks like a smooth ramp, where the wind abrades the rock face. The other side of the boulder looks like a normal rock.

Natural arches, found in several places across the Colorado Plateau of the southeastern United States, occur when the blocks in sandstone cliffs weather. Abrasion by the wind causes the sandstone to erode. Eventually, only a very thin layer of the cliff remains, with a hole under it—forming a natural arch. As a natural arch is being created, the wind-sculpted depressions in the cliff serve as wind caves that provide shelter for small desert animals.

DUNES

When we think of deserts, we think of sand dunes. But not all dunes are made of sand.

Gypsum, an even softer mineral, is a common component of dunes in New Mexico. Black dunes, in regions with volcanic minerals, contain grains of obsidian and basalt. And even dried salt, blowing across level ground near the sea, can pile up into a dune.

Dunes need an anchor. A single blade of deep-rooted grass may start the process. The wind piles up particles against the

These windblown sandstone patterns are in the Paria Wilderness in Arizona.

*White gypsum sand dunes in White Sands National Monument,
New Mexico*

The dunes of the Namib Desert in Namibia, Africa

plant. As the pile grows larger, it traps more particles. The small dune provides a place for more plants to take root, making the dune less prone to blowing away. Although stabilized, the dune will continue to move in the direction toward which the wind is blowing. Ripple marks on the dune are a clue to the usual direction of the wind.

There are many types of dunes. Parabolic dunes are the dunes found along most coastlines. Usually stabilized by sea oats, small trees, or other vegetation, they form a U shape with the open end facing toward the direction in which the wind is blowing. Transverse dunes face the wind in rows, looking like a series of walls guarding the beach. Linear dunes form when the wind blows constantly from one direction. With long, parallel ridges and troughs between them, they look like waves—and can be up to 700 feet (213 m) tall.

Crescent-shaped barchan dunes are the classic desert dunes. They have a long, low slope and drop off a steep lip at the top. Sand constantly falls over the face of the dune as it pushes forward. Barchan dunes are a common sight in the Sahara Desert. But the Namib Desert, in Nambia, contains some of the world's tallest dunes. Because of these dunes' unique microclimate, between a cold sea and the warm African interior, they are blanketed in fog every morning. These dunes reach peaks of 1,300 feet (396 m).

DRIFTING DUST

When the wind deposits vast amounts of dust, fine-grained silt, and clay over a large area, the resulting soil is called loess. The soil, sculpted into interlocking shapes by the wind, is dense and mineral-rich. It makes excellent farmland. Loess covers hilltops and valleys along the Mississippi River and the plains of Ukraine. Much of southern China's farmland is loess that blew in from the Gobi Desert. These deposits are up to 1,000 feet (305 m) thick. The loess deposits of Wisconsin and southern Iowa provide the world's most productive environment for growing wheat, corn, and soybeans.

In the early 1900s, farmers plowing the flat prairies of Texas, Oklahoma, Kansas, and Colorado didn't realize that these grasslands served a very crucial purpose. The soil, while rich in nutrients, is very thin, and the grasses helped to anchor it. Many years of serious drought led to the Dust Bowl, between 1935 and 1938.

This photograph of a house surrounded by dust drifts in Prowers County, Colorado, was taken in 1937. It had been abandoned two years before, at the beginning of the Dust Bowl.

Wind erosion scooped the top 3 feet (1 m) of soil off their farms. Dust piled up in drifts like sand dunes and roared in giant clouds across the landscape. One resident called the worst storm "a tornado running sideways, a boiling wall of dirt, horizon to horizon and several thousand feet high." These massive clouds of dust drifted as far as the Atlantic Ocean, raining down soil on ships 300 miles (483 km) out to sea! While not as severe as during the Dust Bowl, wind erosion continues to be a problem in this region.

48

The agents of erosion—water and wind—keep busy at their work every day. Glaciers grind down through valleys. Sandstorms sweep across the deserts. Streams scour deeper into rocky mountainsides. By comparison, human activity has little overall effect on the erosion of our planet. We certainly can't stop it from happening!

But all human activities have the potential to accelerate erosion. When we walk down a path, our shoes kick up little particles of dirt, setting them up to be carried away by rainfall or wind. When we build a house or pave a road, we change the drainage patterns of the surrounding land, affecting how water carries off soil.

Some activities are more destructive than others. Blasting away mountainsides to build dams. Tunneling into valleys to quarry stone. Dumping massive piles of mine waste. Diverting rivers for irrigation. Clear-cutting forests for development. Each contributes heavily to erosion, either by diverting natural water channels or by adding sediment to streams. And when we accelerate erosion to the point where it affects the climate, destroys biomes (ecological communities), and threatens our food supply, we have to step back and examine what we do. How can we lessen our most negative contributions to erosion?

SOIL: A PRECIOUS RESOURCE

Erosion was such a terrible problem in colonial America that Patrick Henry, the noted patriot, once proclaimed: "He is the greatest patriot who stops the most gullies."

The American colonists had little understanding of how the soil they relied on for crops was formed. Coming from Europe, where logging and overgrazing had ruined many soils long before they were born, the colonists didn't understand the connection between trees and soil. As they cut into the dense forests to carve out their farms, the dead leaves that nourished the soils disappeared. Corn, cotton, and tobacco crops, planted in the same acres time and again, drained essential minerals from the soil. Weakened by overplanting and pounded by rain, the soils washed away down gullies and into streams and rivers.

Several early American conservationists—Jared Elliot, John Bartram, and Samuel Deane among them—studied the problem and made suggestions for plowing techniques and crop rotation that would restore the land. But by 1800, much of the coastal land in both Massachusetts and Connecticut could no longer support crops. In the Piedmont plateau, the low hills from Virginia to Alabama east of the Appalachian Mountains, eroded red clay hills looked like scars across the landscape. As more and more crops failed in the ruined eastern soils, settlers moved farther west, continuing the cycle. But many stayed—and learned how to lessen the erosion of their farmland.

All farming techniques affect how quickly topsoil erodes. If the same crops are planted in the same spot over and over again, they will remove too many critical minerals from the soil. Corn and soybeans drain a lot of minerals from the soil. Patterns of tilling make a difference, too. If a farmer plows fields along the shape of

CROPS AND EROSION

Crop rotation, the practice of growing different crops on the same piece of land, helps prevent erosion. While corn drains the soil of essential nutrients, red clover puts important minerals back in the soil. Other grasses used for hay, such as alfalfa and ryegrass, improve the soil by adding nutrients to it. By switching between such crops, farmers can ensure that the soil doesn't become mineral-depleted and useless for farming.

Contour plowing follows the shape of the land.

the land rather than trying to make straight rows across it, less soil will wash away when it rains. If dead plants are removed instead of plowed under, the soil doesn't have an anchor and may blow away in the wind. But the plowed-under remains of last year's crop restore minerals to the soil, as does the application of manure.

By planting lines of trees as windbreaks, farmers helped keep the wind from picking up loose soil and blowing it away. And by planting bushes in gullies, they fought against the continued erosion of gullies from rainfall.

Without soil, we have no crops—and without crops, we have no food. Keeping nutrient-rich soil from eroding is still a challenge to farmers. It's an essential battle to ensure that the world's rich agricultural regions remain a valuable resource for all of us.

THE IMPORTANCE OF GROUND COVER

In ancient Greece, shipbuilders logged vast forests of oak to build mighty fleets. Without humus to replenish the soil, the weakened soil washed away, leaving expanses of limestone bedrock exposed to the sky. To cultivate the little remaining soil, farmers built terraces on eroded hillsides, creating platforms on which to grow olive trees and grapevines.

In Switzerland, large forests used to protect villages from avalanches and rockslides. Air pollution, logging, and disease killed large numbers of trees. Alpine terrain has very little soil on top of the bedrock, so it's difficult for trees to grow there. As established trees continue to die off, the slopes of the Alps become more prone to erosion—and more dangerous to the people living in the valleys below. Although human-made barriers have been constructed to take their place, the loss of Switzerland's forests mean more erosion, more flooding, and more dangerous avalanches.

When ground cover disappears—through overgrazing, plowing, disease, or logging—the stage is set for erosion to deal a fatal blow. Wind scoops up unanchored soil and carries it away. Rain washes the loose soil into streams, sending it toward the sea. Once the fertile layers of soil are gone, only barren bedrock remains. What was once a prime growing region can no longer support agriculture.

Each acre of land can afford to lose 2 to 5 tons of soil each year. If flooding, severe winds, or heavy rains remove more soil, that piece of land will remain permanently scarred, unable to support plant life. Erosion of this nature occurred thousands of years ago,

52

changing the face of the land forever. Green meadows in Italy and along the Adriatic Sea gave way to barren karst as sheep and goats ate what little ground cover anchored the soil. Cut down for fuel, the lush forests of England are a fading historical footnote. Erosion of this magnitude is now a problem in the Mississippi Valley, the high southwestern Plains states, and many other scattered regions across North America. Can we learn from the past to protect our future?

GLOSSARY

abrasion: when friction generated by wind, water, ice, or movement causes particles to polish or erode surfaces

alluvial fan: loose clay, silt, sand, gravel, and small rocks deposited in a fan shape when a mountain stream drops into a valley

arête: a knife-blade-shaped mountain ridge carved by two glaciers

bedrock: the solid rock layer underneath a layer of soil

biome: a specific biological community, such as a desert or rain forest

blowhole: an eroded seaside hole through which water spouts

blowout: a hollow in the earth's surface created by wind erosion

butte: a flat-topped, steep-sided hill

canyon: a large, long, narrow gorge with deep, steep sides

cavern: a hollow under the earth's surface, carved by erosion

cirque: a deep bowl-shaped formation carved into rock by a glacier

crevasses: deep cracks in the snowpack on top of a glacier

deflation: when wind removes particles from the ground; also wind erosion

delta: sediments deposited at the mouth of a river

deposition: the dropping away of eroded material from its origins

drift: loose material deposited by a glacier

drumlin: a long, narrow mound of sand, gravel, and clay deposited by a glacier, pointing in the direction of the glacier's flow

dune: a small hill that has been piled up by wind action

erosion: the process of water or wind carrying away silt, soil, sand, and rocks

erratic: a boulder carried by a glacier and deposited far from its source

esker: a long, winding hill that develops as sand and gravel deposits build up in layers from streams running under or through a glacier

fjord: a steep-walled, deep coastal valley carved by an outlet glacier

flowstone: a cavern deposit of stone formed by the flow of mineral-rich water over surfaces

glacier: a large mass of ice and snow flowing downhill under its own weight

gorge: a deep, steep-sided valley carved by stream erosion

gully: a deep channel formed by the merger of many sources of rainwater runoff

hanging valley: a glacial valley at a high elevation, ending in midair

headland: a cliff sticking out far into the sea, where it can be attacked by waves on many sides

helictite: a curved stalactite

hoodoo: a column of stone, often larger at the top, shaped by wind erosion

humus: the decomposed remains of plants and animals

ice cap: a sheet of ice covering a large area, created by the constant accumulation of snow

iceberg: a huge piece of ice that breaks off the end of an outlet glacier and floats away

igneous: relating to rock formed by volcanic forces

joint: a natural fracture between layers of rock

kame: a steep-sided hill of sand, gravel, and clay dropped in layers by a glacier

karst: a landscape where the bedrock dissolves easily, allowing erosion to form sink-holes and caverns

kettle lake: a lake hollowed out by and filled with glacial ice that melted in place

loess: fine silt carried by the wind and deposited in layers

matterhorn: a pyramid-shaped mountain peak carved on three sides by glaciers

mesa: a flat-topped mountain with at least one steep side

metamorphic: relating to rock formed by heat or pressure

moraine: a long ridge of rock and soil that develops inside a glacier

natural arch: an arch of sandstone formed when blocks of sandstone weather and erode out of a canyon wall

natural bridge: an arch of stone caused by water eroding away the underlying rock

pedestal: a column of stone, shaped by wind erosion

pinnacle: a slender column of rock

pothole: a rounded hole eroded into the underlying rock of a streambed

riegel: gigantic terraces created on a mountainside by a glacier's retreat

rill: a tiny path carved in the soil by rainwater flowing downhill

rock flour: fine silt that a glacier creates by grinding into the rocks along the sides of a valley

sea stack: a pillar of resistant rock along a coastline, left behind as the coastline retreats

sedimentary: relating to rock formed by deposition of eroded pieces of preexisting rocks

sinkhole: a depression in the earth's surface formed by either the erosion of under-lying bedrock or the collapse of a cavern roof

soil: a mixture of silt, sand, clay, and humus

stalactite: a cavern deposit created by mineral-rich water dripping from the roof of a cave

stalagmite: a cavern deposit formed when mineral-rich water drips off a stalactite and builds up from the floor of a cave

stream load: suspended silt, sand, and rock fragments that do most of the work of stream erosion

ventifact: desert boulders shaped on one side like a smooth ramp by wind erosion

weathering: the chemical and physical processes of breaking up rocks

RECOMMENDED RESOURCES

FURTHER READING

Bender, Lionel. *Heat and Drought.* Raintree Steck-Vaughn, 1998.

Catherall, Ed. *Exploring Soil and Rocks.* Steck-Vaughn Co., 1991.

Gallant, Roy A. *The Ice Ages.* Franklin-Watts, 1985.

Graham, Ada and Frank. *The Changing Desert.* Charles Scribner's Sons, 1981.

Markle, Sandra. *Earth Alive.* Lothrop, Lee, and Shepard Books, 1991.

Ocko, Stephanie. *Water: Almost Enough for Everyone.* Atheneum Books for Young Readers, 1995.

Parker, Steve. *Eyewitness Books: Seashore.* Alfred A. Knopf, 1989.

ON THE WORLD WIDE WEB

The Internet changes constantly, so you never know what you'll find next. Try these sites for more information on erosion, and use a search engine with keywords like "wind erosion," "water erosion," "stream erosion," and "weathering" to dig up some more.

The Day of the Black Blizzard
www.discovery.com/area/history/dustbowl/dustbowl1.1.html
The drama and terror of the worst dust storm of the Dust Bowl. Includes video and links to other Dust Bowl sites. Presented by the Discovery Channel.

Deserts Field Trip
www.fieldguides.com/desert/desert.htm
A collection of information about deserts, where you can visit and learn about deserts around the world. By Tramline Web Tours.

EarthShots: Satellite Images of Environmental Change
edcwww.cr.usgs.gov/earthshots/slow/tableofcontents
See how human activity worldwide—especially agriculture and logging—has affected the environments we live in. Provided by the U.S. Geological Survey.

The Glacier Project Homepage
www.glacier.rice.edu/
Learn about continental glaciers on the coldest continent on earth. From Rice University.

National Speleological Society
www.caves.org
The world's largest organization of researchers devoted to studying caverns. You don't have to be a scientist to join—you just have to love caves.

The South Pole Web Adventure Page
www.southpole.com/
How cold is it at the South Pole? Look here to find out, and to ask questions of scientists who work on the Antarctic ice cap. By Bishop Web Works.

The Virtual Cave
www.goodearth.com/virtcave.html
Explore the dark and beautiful world of cave formations. From Good Earth Graphics.

AMAZING LANDSCAPES

Erosion has shaped some incredible landscapes all across our planet. If you can't visit them in person, be sure to track them down on the Internet.

NORTH AMERICA

Arches National Park, Utah
www.nps.gov/arch/
This park has more natural arches than anywhere else in the world, including the world's largest arch—Landscape Arch. It sweeps 291 feet (89 m) across the canyon floor.

Badlands National Park, South Dakota
www.nps.gov/badl/
A sea of strange rock formations eroded by wind and rain, the Badlands contain arches, hoodoos, jagged ridges, and pyramid-shaped peaks.

Banff National Park, Alberta
www.worldweb.com/parkscanada-banff/index.html
Canada's first national park features active glaciers, glacial features, deep canyons, and hoodoos.

Bruce Peninsula National Park, Ontario
parkscanada.pch.gc.ca/parks/ontario/bruce_peninsula/bruce_peninsulae.htm
Eroded limestone formations—including many caves—crowd the coastline of the Niagara Escarpment along Georgian Bay. Flowerpots, similar to sea stacks, rise from the deep water off Flowerpot Island.

Bryce Canyon National Park, Utah
www.nps.gov/brca/
Colorful pinnacles of eroded limestone
and sandstone soar over the desert
floor. Bryce has 50 miles (80 km) of
hiking trails that zigzag through rock
mazes and past hoodoos.

Cacahuamilpa Caves, Taxco, Mexico
www.acavio.com/cacahuamilpa-
grottos.htm
Twenty huge chambers—up to 131 feet
(40 m) tall—fill 1.5 square miles (3.9 sq
km) of this massive cavern network.
There are at least 44 miles (71 km) of
known passageways, of which 6 miles
(10 km) have been fully explored.

Canyonlands National Park, Utah
www.nps.gov/cany/
In the high desert country of Utah,
Canyonlands encompasses a vast
network of slot canyons, deep gorges,
mesas, buttes, and other wind- and
water-eroded sandstone formations.

Cape Breton Highlands, Nova Scotia
parkscanada.pch.gc.ca/parks/nova_scotia
/cape_highlands/cape_highlandse.htm
Massive cliffs, eroded by the sea, are
protected within this Atlantic coastal
park.

Carlsbad Caverns National Park, New
Mexico
www.nps.gov/cave/
More than seventy caves make up this
network of caverns underneath the
Guadalupe Mountains. Known for its
immense chambers, Carlsbad boasts
"The Big Room"—4,270 feet (1,301 m)
long, 636 feet (194 m) wide, and tall
enough to fit a 28-story skyscraper.

Denali National Park, Alaska
www.nps.gov/dena/
At 20,320 feet (6,194 m) above sea
level, Mount McKinley (Denali) is
North America's highest peak. Valley

glaciers crawl down its slopes in every
direction, feeding streams, rivers, and
lakes with melting glacial ice. Its longest
glacial flow is nearly 35 miles (56 km)
long.

Fundy National Park, Canada
parkscanada.pch.gc.ca/parks/new_brun
swick/fundy/fundye.htm
Rugged cliffs along the Bay of Fundy
provide a place to watch the world's
highest tides—rising 52 feet (16 m).

Glacier Bay National Park and
Preserve, Alaska
www.nps.gov/glba/
Cruise ships, sea kayaks, and planes are
the only transportation to this unusual
national park, where numerous outlet
glaciers constantly calve icebergs into
the cold sea.

Glacier National Park, British
Columbia
www.harbour.com/parkscan/glacier/
More than 400 glaciers swarm down
from the peaks of the Columbia
Mountains.

Glacier National Park, Montana
www.nps.gov/glac/
Touching the border with Canada, this
park has more than sixty glaciers—and
1,000 miles (1,609 km) of hiking trails
where you can explore glacially carved
terrain. Arêtes, matterhorns, and
glacial valleys dominate the landscape.
Small glaciers continue to creep down
some of the higher peaks, creating
beautiful turquoise lakes with their
melting ice.

Grand Canyon National Park, Arizona
www.nps.gov/grca/
The Colorado River winds along for
277 miles (446 km) in its eroded
course, 6,000 feet (1,829 m) deep
through the world's most spectacular
canyon.

Grand Staircase–Escalante National Monument, Utah

www.desertusa.com/escalante/index.html
A wilderness region encompassing 14,844 square miles (38,446 sq km) of cliffs, plateaus, windswept sandstone formations, and slot canyons.

Grand Teton National Park, Wyoming

www.nps.gov/grte/
The towering arêtes and matterhorns of the Grand Tetons show the effects of glacial erosion on the youngest mountains in the Rockies.

Great Sand Dunes National Monument, Colorado

www.nps.gov/grsa/
The tallest sand dunes in North America aren't anywhere near a shoreline. Instead, they collected at the base of the Sangre de Cristo Mountains. The wind carries sand from a nearby desert, the San Luis Valley. When the wind hits the mountains, it drops the sand. These dunes are up to 600 feet (183 m) tall.

Hells Canyon, Idaho

www.ohwy.com/id/h/hellcnra.htm
Hells Canyon's deepest point is 7,900 feet (2,408 m), making it the deepest river gorge in North America. Carved by the Snake River, this narrow canyon cuts through basalt, an ancient volcano rock that erodes very slowly.

Huasteca Canyon, Nueva Leon, Mexico

www.geocities.com/Yosemite/3921/huasteca.htm
Deep in the eastern Sierra Madre, the Huasteca River carved this steep-walled canyon of bare rock, 1,000 feet (305 m) tall. The "Grand Canyon of Mexico" is a favorite destination for rock climbers.

Jasper National Park, Alberta

www.worldweb.com/parkscanada-jasper/index.html
The Athabasca glacier, a remnant of the last ice age, makes up part of the Columbia Icefield in the Canadian Rockies. At this park, you can tour the glacier and look into crevasses more than 130 feet (40 m) deep.

Kenai Fjords National Park, Alaska

www.nps.gov/kefj/
South of Anchorage, this park allows you to walk along a glacier and an ice field. Boat trips take visitors into the fjord.

Mammoth Cave National Park, Kentucky

www.nps.gov/maca/
More than 336 miles (541 km) of passageways make Mammoth Cave the world's largest explored cave system.

Mount Rainier National Park, Washington

www.nps.gov/mora/
Eleven glaciers creep down the sides of Mount Rainier, a dormant volcano that rises 14,410 feet (4,392 m) in the Cascade Range. Moraines, glacial lakes, and ice caves are accessible by hiking trails during the summer.

Natural Bridges National Monument, Utah

www.nps.gov/nabr/
This park protects three large natural bridges. Two of them are the world's second- and third-largest.

Niagara Falls, Ontario/New York

www.iaw.com/~falls/
One of the world's largest waterfalls, spilling 1.5 million gallons (5.7 million liters) of water per second over three cataracts—Horseshoe Falls, American Falls, and Bridal Veil Falls.

Olympic National Park, Washington

www.nps.gov/olym/
In the middle of the glacier-rich Olympic Mountains, Mount Olympus

rises 7,965 feet (2,428 m) high. Six glaciers flow down its slopes. Dozens of sea stacks line the park's coast.

Pinnacles National Monument, New Mexico
www.nps.gov/pinn/
Pinnacles of stone, rising up to 1,200 feet (366 m), are the highlight of this park.

Rainbow Bridge National Park, New Mexico
www.nps.gov/rabr/
The world's largest natural bridge—290 feet (88 m) tall, 275 feet (84 m) long, and 33 feet (10 m) wide at the top—this geological formation is a sacred spot for the Navajo Indians.

Sequoia National Park, California
www.nps.gov/seki/
The jagged peaks of Mount Whitney—the tallest mountain in the continental United States at 14,495 feet (4,418 m)—are home to Tulainyo Lake, a water-filled cirque that is the highest lake in the United States.

Sleeping Bear Sand Dunes National Lakeshore, Michigan
www.nps.gov/slbe/
Along Lake Michigan, 35 miles (56 km) of shoreline contain dunes that sweep up to 200 feet (61 m) tall. The park also contains ancient glacial features such as moraines and kettle lakes.

Yosemite National Park, California
www.nps.gov/yose/
Glaciers once carved this section of the Sierra Nevada mountain range, leaving behind deep glacial valleys. Waterfalls plunge off the edges of high hanging valleys. Yosemite's unusual Half Dome peak is a mountain cut in two by a glacier.

Zion National Park, Utah
www.nps.gov/zion/
In addition to sweeping cliffs and deep canyons, this park contains the world's largest natural arch—Kolob Arch, spanning 310 feet (94 m).

WORLDWIDE

Aletsch Glacier, Switzerland
www.artfurrer.ch/sommer/aletschge.htm
Longest, largest glacier in the Alps.

Angel Falls, Venezuela
www2.planeta.com/mader/planeta/0897/0897canaima.html
The world's highest waterfall. It falls 3,212 feet (979 m) from the top of a strangely eroded mountain—a tepui.

Ayers Rock, or Uluru, Australia
www.cco.caltech.edu/~salmon/wh-uluru.html
One of only two sandstone mountains rising above Australia's barren desert outback is 2 miles (3.2 km) across and 1,100 feet (335 m) tall.

Colca River Canyon, Peru
www.peru-explorer.com/colca.htm
South America's deepest canyon—10,500 feet (3,200 m) deep and 236 miles (380 km) long.

Fjordland National Park, New Zealand
newzealand.com/MilfordTrack/index.html
A World Heritage Park including fjords, glaciers, glacial features—and a rain forest.

Iguazú Falls, South America
darkwing.uoregon.edu/~sergiok/brasil/iguacu.html
Straddling the border between Brazil and Argentina, these falls sweep in a wide arc almost 2 miles (3.2 km) long.

Sogne Fjord, Norway
www.franksgrafikk.no/val_sogn/
indexsog.htm
Norway's deepest, longest fjord—120
miles (193 km) long and 4,000 feet
(1,219 m) deep.

Torres de Paine, Patagonia, Chile
www.gorp.com/gorp/location/latamer/
chile/paine.htm
Some of the world's youngest mountains, these continue to be carved by
glaciers. Nearby is the Messier Channel,
the world's deepest fjord—4,226 feet
(1,288 m) deep.

Vatnajökull, Iceland
www.ismennt.is/vefir/earth/mhpub/
netdays/nd8.htm
Two major volcanoes lurk under this
continental glacier, covering 3,205
square miles (8,301 sq km). When the
volcanoes erupt, they melt the ice, creating some of the world's largest floods.

Victoria Falls, Zambia
www.gorp.com/gorp/location/africa/
zimbabwe/victoria.htm
Africa's most dramatic waterfall,
pushing 15 million gallons (57 million
liters) of water per minute over a
cascade more than a mile wide.

Vikos Gorge, Greece
www.uoi.gr/metsovo/10vicos/vicos.htm
Eroded through limestone karst
bedrock, the steep gorge is more than
3,000 feet (912 m) deep.

Yunnan Rock Forest, China
www.sh.com/china/travel/scenery/
scene15.htm
A scenic tropical karst landscape of
eroded limestone mountains, so close
together that they look like a field of
gumdrops.

INDEX

63